Blastoff! Readers are carefully developed by literacy experts to build reading stamina and move students toward fluency by combining standards-based content with developmentally appropriate text.

 Level 1 provides the most support through repetition of high-frequency words, light text, predictable sentence patterns, and strong visual support.

 Level 2 offers early readers a bit more challenge through varied sentences, increased text load, and text-supportive special features.

 Level 3 advances early-fluent readers toward fluency through increased text load, less reliance on photos, advancing concepts, longer sentences, and more complex special features.

★ **Blastoff! Universe**

Reading Level

 Grade K →  Grades 1–3 →  Grade 4

This edition first published in 2026 by Bellwether Media, Inc.

No part of this publication may be reproduced in whole or in part without written permission of the publisher. For information regarding permission, write to Bellwether Media, Inc., Attention: Permissions Department, 3500 American Blvd W, Suite 150, Bloomington, MN 55431.

Library of Congress Cataloging-in-Publication Data

LC record for Barges available at: https://lccn.loc.gov/2025010712

Text copyright © 2026 by Bellwether Media, Inc. BLASTOFF! READERS and associated logos are trademarks and/or registered trademarks of Bellwether Media, Inc. Bellwether Media is a division of FlutterBee Education Group.

Editor: Suzane Nguyen   Designer: Jeffrey Kollock

Printed in the United States of America, North Mankato, MN.

Table of Contents

What Are Barges?	4
All Hands on Deck!	12
Massive Movers	20
Glossary	22
To Learn More	23
Index	24

What Are Barges?

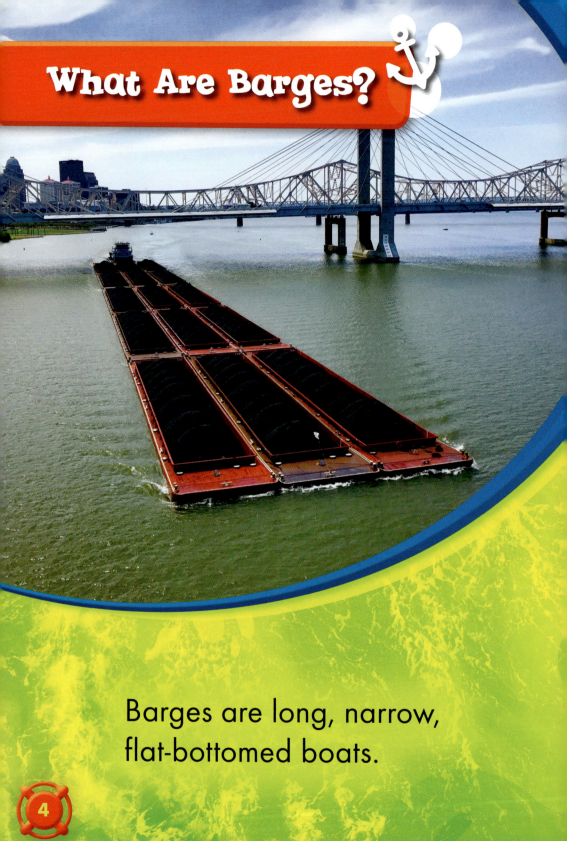

Barges are long, narrow, flat-bottomed boats.

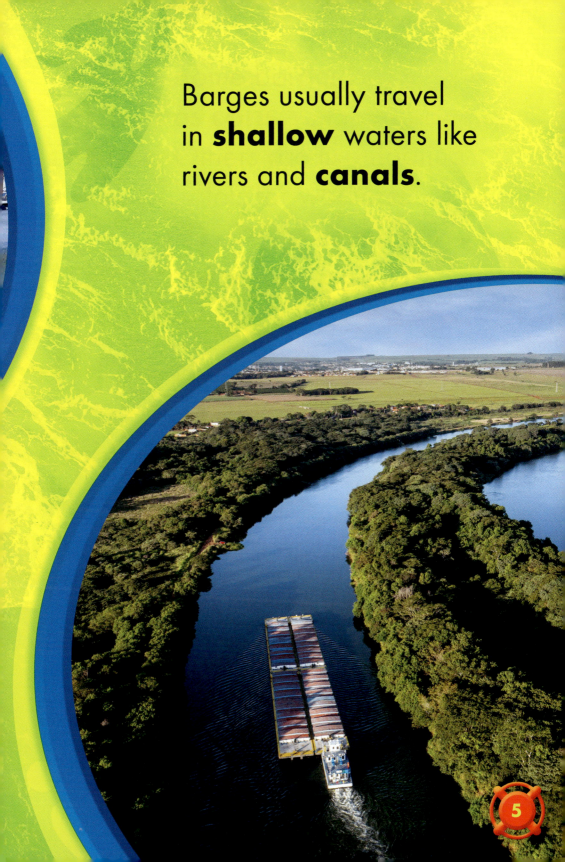

Barges usually travel in **shallow** waters like rivers and **canals**.

A barge's **hull** is underwater. This is what makes the barge float.

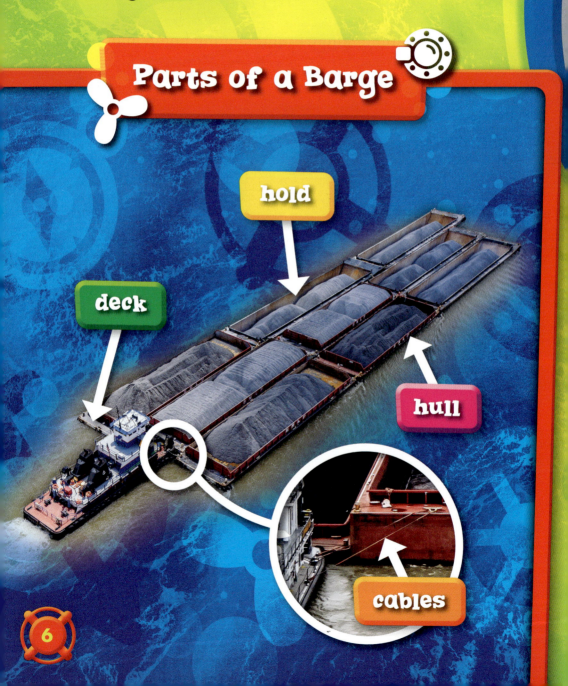

Parts of a Barge

- hold
- deck
- hull
- cables

Most barges cannot move on their own. **Tugboats** pull them. **Cables** help tugboats move many barges at once!

Many barges carry different types of **cargo** on their **deck**.

Cargo can also be placed in a barge's **hold**.

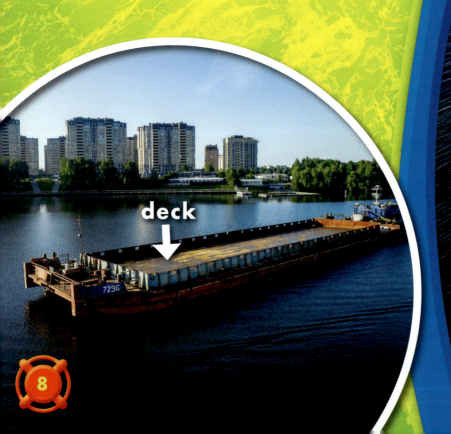
deck

crane barge

Deck barges carry things like building materials and animals. **Crane** barges have a crane to lift cargo.

Types of Barges

deck barge

crane barge

hopper barge

Hopper barges have large bins. They can carry coal, sand, sugar, and more.

All Hands on Deck!

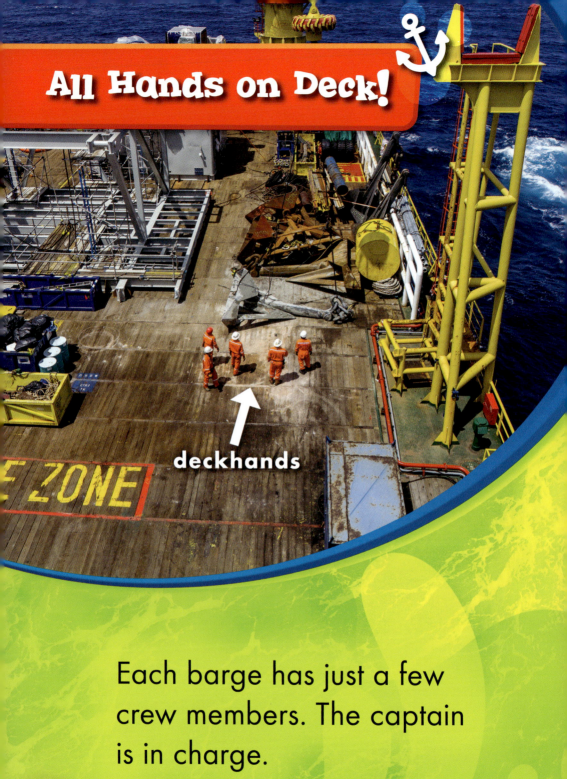

deckhands

Each barge has just a few crew members. The captain is in charge.

Deckhands make sure the barge and its cargo are clean and safe.

Ship Stats

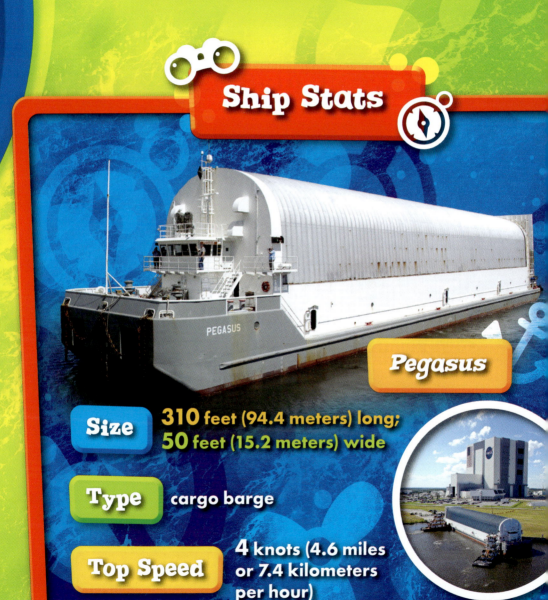

Pegasus

Size	310 feet (94.4 meters) long; 50 feet (15.2 meters) wide
Type	cargo barge
Top Speed	4 knots (4.6 miles or 7.4 kilometers per hour)
Purpose	carry NASA rocket parts

A barge's pilot uses a radio. They talk to the captain of the tugboat.

How Barges Move

1 Cables connect the barges together.

2 Cables connect the tugboat to the barges.

3 The tugboat moves the barges up and down rivers.

4 The tugboat moves the barges into the dock.

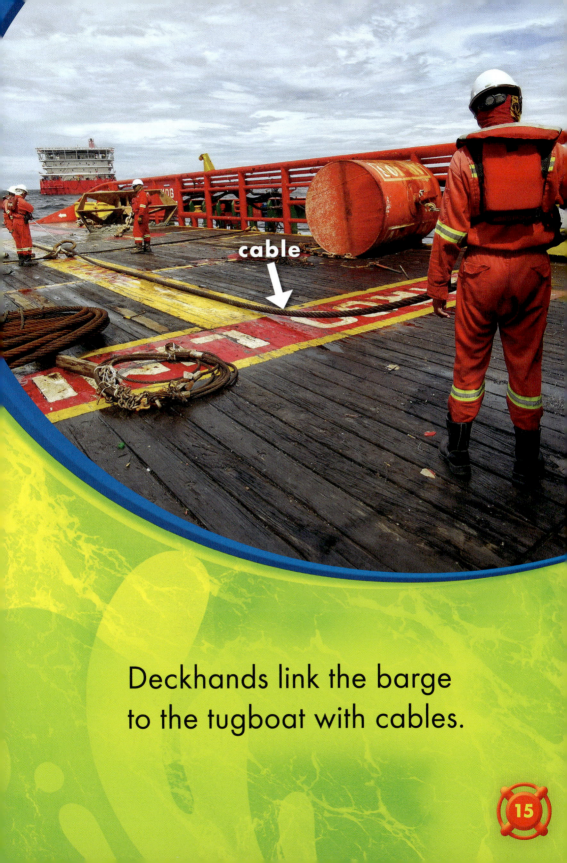

cable

Deckhands link the barge to the tugboat with cables.

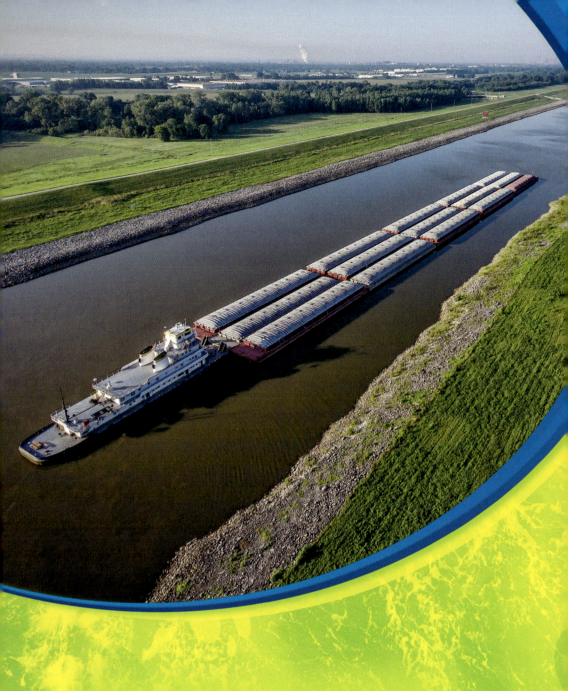

Barges move very slowly. Their trips can last weeks.

Some barges are used as **construction sites**. Others are like floating hotels for workers.

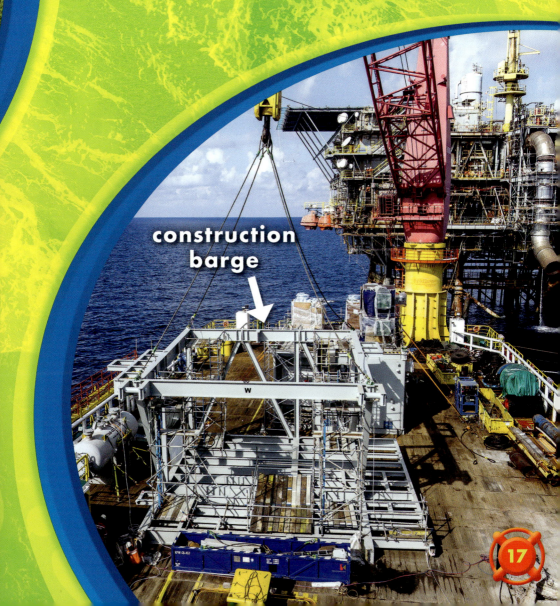

construction barge

Barges are loaded and unloaded at **docks**.

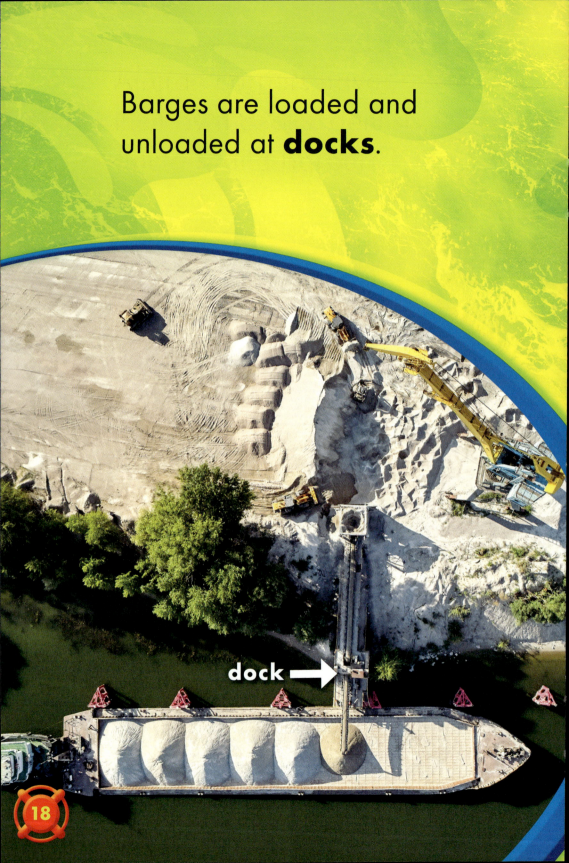

dock →

Dock workers use machines and trucks to move the cargo.

Massive Movers

Trucks, trains, and planes all move cargo. Barges carry even bigger loads.

Barges can be cheaper, too. They help save money on the things we need!

Glossary

cables—steel wires that are twisted together to form strong ropes

canals—human-made waterways that connect to other bodies of water

cargo—goods carried across land, water, or air

construction sites—places or areas where something is built

crane—a machine used to lift and move heavy loads

deck—a flat part on the top of a ship

docks—places where ships are loaded and unloaded

hold—a large area below a ship's deck that is used to store cargo

hull—the main body of a ship

shallow—not deep

tugboats—small, powerful boats that move other ships

To Learn More

AT THE LIBRARY

Crestodina, Tom. *Working Boats: An Inside Look at Ten Amazing Watercraft.* Seattle, Wash.: Sasquatch Books, 2022.

Duling, Kaitlyn. *Container Ships.* Minneapolis, Minn.: Bellwether Media, 2026.

Rathburn, Betsy. *A Ship's Day.* Minneapolis, Minn.: Bellwether Media, 2024.

ON THE WEB

FACTSURFER

Factsurfer.com gives you a safe, fun way to find more information.

1. Go to www.factsurfer.com.

2. Enter "barges" into the search box and click 🔍.

3. Select your book cover to see a list of related content.

Index

cables, 7, 15
canals, 5
captain, 12, 14
cargo, 8, 9, 10, 13, 19, 20
construction sites, 17
crane barges, 10
crew, 12
deck, 8
deck barges, 10
deckhands, 12, 13, 15
docks, 18, 19
hold, 8, 9
hopper barges, 11
hull, 6, 7
move, 7, 14, 16, 19, 20
parts of a barge, 6
Pegasus, 13
pilot, 14
radio, 14
rivers, 5

trucks, 19, 20
tugboats, 7, 14, 15
types, 11
workers, 17, 19

The images in this book are reproduced through the courtesy of: Justin Wilkens, front cover, pp. 1, 21; Ibenk.88, p. 3; David, p. 4; jrslompo, p. 5; Tak, p. 6; Jonathan Dakin, p. 6 (cables); Eric Buermeyer, p. 7; william87, p. 7 (inset); Shaplov Evgeny, p. 8; Stanislav Ostranitsa, p. 9; Artem, p. 10; LuYago, p. 11 (deck barge); GVictoria, p. 11 (crane barge); Raoyang Yang, p. 11 (hopper barge); wanfahmy, pp. 12, 17; Kim Shiflett/ Wikimedia Commons, p. 13; Mike Downs/ Wikimedia Commons, p. 13 (inset); Jim West/ Alamy Stock Photo, p. 14 (1); Rudzenka, p. 14 (2); Igor Groshev, p. 14 (3); Muan Sibero, p. 14 (4); rusdi sembak, p. 15; MarekPhotoDesign.com, p. 16; sarymsakov.com, p. 18; arikbintang, p. 19; portumen, p. 20; Stanislav Komogorov, p. 23.